Yet at the Gates, a Refuge
of Sunflowers and Milkweed

Yet at the Gates, a Refuge of Sunflowers and Milkweed

Dan Williams

ISBN: 978-1-942956-90-7
Library of Congress Control Number: 2021940711
Manufactured in the United States

Lamar University Literary Press
Beaumont, Texas

For friends I deeply miss, whose presence remains in my life;
For friends whose presence sustain my life;
And for Cynthia and Leah, who remain the pillars in my life.

Recent Poetry from Lamar University Literary Press

Bobby Aldridge, *An Affair of the Stilled Heart*
Michael Baldwin, *Lone Star Heart, Poems of a Life in Texas*
Charles Behlen, *Failing Heaven*
David Bowles, *Flower, Song, Dance: Aztec and Mayan Poetry*
Jerry Bradley, *Crownfeathers and Effigies*
Jerry Bradley and Ulf Kirchdorfer, editors, *The Great American
    Wise Ass Poetry Anthology*
Jerry Bradley, *Collapsing into Possibility*
Matthew Brennan, *One Life*
Julie Chappel, *Mad Habits of a Life*
Chip Dameron, *Waiting for an Etcher*
William Virgil Davis, *The Bones Poems*
Jeffrey DeLotto, *Voices Writ in Sand*
Chris Ellery, *Elder Tree*
Larry Griffin, *Cedar Plums*
Ken Hada, *Margaritas and Redfish*
Katherine Hoerth, *Goddess Wears Cowboy Boots*
Lynn Hoggard, *Motherland*
Godspower Oboido, *Wandering Feet on Pebbled Shores*
Gretchen Johnson, *A Trip Through Downer, Minnesota*
Ulf Kirchdorfer, *Chewing Green Leaves*
Laozi, *Daodejing*, tr. By David Breeden, Steven Schroeder, and
    Wally Swist
Janet McCann, *The Crone at the Casino*
Laurence Musgrove, *Local Bird*
Dave Oliphant, *The Pilgrimage, Selected Poems: 1962-2012*
Kornelijus Platelis, *Solitary Architectures*
Carol Coffee Reposa, *Underground Musicians*
Jan Seale, *The Parkinson Poems*
Jan Seale, *A Lifetime of Words*
Jan Seale, *Particulars*
Glen Sorestad *Hazards of Eden*
W.K. Stratton, *Ranchero Ford/ Dying in Red Dirt Country*
W. K. Stratton, *Colo-State-Pen: 18456, A Dark Miscellany*
W. K Stratton, *Betrayal Creek*
Loretta Diane Walker, *Desert Light*
Dan Williams, *Past Purgatory, A Distant Paradise*
Wally Swist, *Invocation*
Jonas Zdanys (ed.), *Pushing the Envelope, Epistolary Poems*
Jonas Zdanys, *Red Stones*
Jonas Zdanys, *Three White Horses*

For information on these and other LULP books go to
www.Lamar.edu/literarypress

Acknowledgments

The list of those who have helped and encouraged me is endless, and I am humbled by considering by their gracious support. From the moment we met at a Texas Book Festival, Jerry Craven has continually been both a good friend and advocate for my writing. I also gratefully acknowledge the encouragement I received from Jim Hoggard, one of the truly great Texan poets, who sadly passed this year, from Lynn Hoggard, Sherry Craven, Karla and Alan, Jerry Bradley, Katherine Hoerth, Jim Sanderson, Gerald Duff, Hank O'Neal, Laurence Musgrove, the entire Langdon crowd, and so many fellow writers from TACWT. I am also indebted to so many friends on campus and as well to my colleagues here at TCU Press. Heartful thanks to you all.

Other Books by Dan Williams include

You Can't Build a Company
Past Purgatory, A Distant Paradise
The Lords of Absence
The Lords of Leftovers
*8 Voices: Contemporary Poetry from the American
    Southwest*
*Pillars of Salt: An Anthology of Early American Criminal
    Narratives*

CONTENTS

Virgin Martyrs, The Most Poetical Topic

Resurrected by a dumb bird squawking
"Nevermore," the poet, perpetually plagued
by the imp of the perverse, the pursuit
of the inaccessible, proclaimed, "The death
of a beautiful woman is, unquestionably,
the most poetical topic in the world."
Sanctifying insufferable suffering, those

early church fathers, venerable patriarchs
of purity and morality, found an abundance
of poetical subjects, scores of holy virgin
martyrs, innocents in agony, condemned
to endure dreadful torments and afflictions,
beautiful young women, untouched and pure,
tortured, disfigured, and murdered most

horribly for embracing Christ their lover,
their stories and bones venerated, ossified
 knuckles and toes consecrated, the worship
of hallowed saints, relics, pain, and virginity.
The chronicles of martyrs are blotted with
poetical topics, the sanctified blood of virgins,
their pages splattered with dreadful death.

Juliana, for example, having wedded Christ,
refused to marry Eleusius, the man her father
chose, a proud pagan provost, giver of laws,
her father Africanus, unknowing his daughter's
secret baptism, her vow of perpetual chastity,
and hostile to Christians, beat her savagely
for defying his will, then ceded her to Eleusius,

who ordered Juliana stretched between pillars
and doused with molten metal. Refusing
to renounce, she was imprisoned, and a devil,
the son of Beelzebub, appeared at her trial,
a surprise witness, before the implacable
provost, who had his betrothed beheaded.
Dorothy, a beautiful maiden from Cappadocia,

was desired by Fabricus, another pagan provost,
but spurned his offer of marriage; scorned
and disgruntled, he cast her in jail, where angels
nourished her, he cast her into boiling oil,
which miraculously transformed into balm,
he stretched her on an iron bed over flames,
which made her smile, indignant, he had her

beheaded, in the lives of saints, Dorothy is
celebrated as patroness of brides, brewers,
gardeners, midwives, and newlyweds, and she is
invoked against fire, lightning, and thieves.
Pope Urban VIII built a church to honor the virgin
martyr Martina, under whose protection he
placed Rome, as she had miraculously survived

 being flogged with iron hooks, being showered
with boiling grease, being thrown to the lions,
and being burned at the stake, all while praising
her lover Christ; when beheaded, not blood, but
a fountain of milk gushed her severed neck,
a miracle so astounding her executioners converted.
A noble Sicilian virgin, Agatha snubbed the advances

of Quintianus, a Roman senator, who spitefully ordered
her breasts cut off, but Saint Peter appeared in her cell,
applying celestial salves to her wounds, restoring her
mammary glands, Agatha was imprisoned in a bawdy
house with Aphrodesia and her six shameless daughters,
but survived *intacta*, and then survived being burned
at the stake, a sudden volcanic eruption disrupting

the proceedings, patroness of wet nurses, she is invoked
against breast disease, fires, and volcanic eruptions.
Patroness of virgins and girl scouts, Agnes was thirteen
years old when, disdaining love gifts she rejected all
her ardent lovers, including Eutropius, the Governor's
son, declaring: "I have chosen a Spouse who cannot be
seen with mortal eyes, whose mouth drips with milk

and honey," when threatened with the tools of torture,
and the Governor's pitiless wrath, she proclaimed, "You
will soon learn that my God is a God of purity. He will
bring your wicked purpose to naught." The heartless
Governor ordered her stripped naked, then led through
the streets to a brothel, yet miraculously, as she stepped
into the street, her golden hair grew, concealing her

shame, and once inside the den of iniquity, an angel
appeared, clothing her in a shining white garment,
her only customer, Eutropius, was either struck blind
or dead (accounts vary) when he reached lewdly
for her, but the saintly Agnes cured him, a kindness
resulting in her being condemned for witchcraft
and burned, stabbed, or beheaded (accounts again

vary), Saint Ambrose, who was not present, declared,
when led to her death, "She went more cheerfully
than others go to their weddings." A most venerated
virgin martyr, Saint Barbara, credited with thirteen
miracles in the fifteenth century, though her martyrdom,
supposedly, took place in the third century (the early
Church fathers fail to mention her), was revered

as one of the Fourteen Holy Helpers for saving
helpless sufferers from the Black Death, Dioscorus
her father her despoiler, a covetous pagan, kept her
locked in a tower, jealous of her purity; when she
acknowledged her faith, he drew his sword to kill
her, yet miraculously the tower wall cracked open,
and she was transported to a mountain gorge, but

a pagan shepherd soon betrayed her (the shepherd
turned to stone, his sheep turned into locusts), and her
father her pursuer dragged her before the pagan
prefect, who tortured her, yet miraculously the dark
prison was bathed in light every night, and every
morning her wounds were healed, unrelenting,
the prefect ordered her beheading, and her father

her destroyer severed daughter from life, yet
miraculously, on his way home, her father
was struck by lightning and consumed by flame.
Christiana, Justina, Margaret, Cecilia, Apollonia, Macra,
and more, all beautiful Christian maidens tortured
by pagan men, all brides of Christ, all the most
poetical subjects enshrined, relics of virginal purity.

The World's Greatest Influencer, Johannes Gensfleisch

His family name means goose meat, but everyone
knows him by his place name, though little is known
about his life, and his grave's lost, he's regarded
as one of the most significant figures in human
history, there's scores of statues, paintings,
stamps, books, and medallions honoring him, too
many to count, there's a university named after

him, and a museum, two operas, even an asteroid,
with no apparent irony the world's oldest
digital library and an online editing system
also bear his name, and the A&E Network
ranked him No. 1, the most influential person
of the second millennium, and just today
he was celebrated in a Google Doodle, yet

his life, what's known, was marked by stops
and starts, sudden moves of occupations
and locations, accused of misusing borrowed
funds, a devastating lawsuit crushed his life,
his property seized by betrayal, leaving him
bankrupt, never to recover, he was a minter
a goldsmith, a gem-polisher, and was involved

in a scheme to sell pilgrims polished metal
mirrors capable of capturing the divine light
emitted by religious relics, he was a printer
who mixed lead, tin, and antimony to create his
own type, and a process for mass-producing
moveable type, he developed oil-based ink,
and adjustable molds, and adapted agricultural

screw presses used for making wine to print
his books, rather than the Bible, he first printed
a poem, and then thousands of indulgences,
a most profitable business, and within a year
of printing 180 Bibles, or so, his creditor sued
and was awarded his property, his Bible printing
workshop, and half the printed Bibles, it's not

known what books he published, as none carry
his name, yet the Bibles, those that remain,
are among the most valuable of all books,
works of delicate, painstaking art, Gutenberg
launched a revolution that lasted five centuries,
the age of print, the era of mass communication,
the spread of literacy, the rise of the middle

class, the Renaissance, Reformation, Scientific
Revolution, Enlightenment, the rise of vernacular
languages, the decline of Latin—all are attributed
to him, universally known yet little known, a schemer,
a dreamer, he might have published Aventur und Kunst,
a mysterious book, revealing the secrets of his craft.

John the Grammarian, When Religion Was Magic

Not to be confused with two other
Johns, also Grammarians, men known
for their learning, erudite scholars
of enigmatic knowledge, John VII
was Patriarch of Constantinople
for half a dozen years in the ninth
century, a time when religion was

magic, and early Christians fervently
believed in the potency of icons,
relics, rituals, amulets, saints, spells,
prayers, potions, and healing stones
to perform miracles, onyx, for example,
prevented miscarriages and cleansed
the female body of corruption, this

otherworldly world, where natural
merged with preternatural, where evil
spirits bedeviled all, where people deathly
ill, hopelessly hoping, chained themselves
to churches, where pagan statues were
alive with the power to kill or cure,
where ripples of water in delicate bowls,

lecanomancy, foretold future events,
and astrology, the reading of stars, was
the Word of God, an iconoclast, John
could have been known as The Hammer,
The Cleaner, the Destroyer of Statues,
though the inaccuracies of sources
precludes exact knowing, he smashed

statues, cleaned the clutter, the idolatry,
railed against stoicheiosis, statue magic,
and apotropaic, counter magic, and led
the second wave of Byzantine iconoclasm,
until a relative, wife of his patron, loving
idols more than family, deposed him, then
two centuries later another scholar, John

Skylitzes, attacked the toppled Patriarch,
accusing him of evil sorcery, of conjuring
power from the statues he destroyed, once
powerful, a sage of God's holy fire, surrounded
by gold mosaics and radiant designs thought
eternal, mere moments of magnificence,
Byzantium was no country for old men.

Cosmas and Damian, Two Sets of Two Heads

Nothing's known about their lives,
just their deaths, Cosmas and Damian,
martyred saints, patrons of barbers,
hairdressers, doctors, surgeons,
dentists, druggists, and probably
veterinarians, twins from Arabia,
healers who never charged a fee,

adored as "the moneyless ones,"
"the silverless," the unmercenaries,"
the brothers incubated the sick,
isolating them in churches at night
to await dream cures, their most
famous healing, grafting a black
leg onto a white body, or perhaps

a white leg onto a black body,
depending on the story, in Syria,
under the persecution of Emperor
Diocletian, they were martyred,
first tortured to recant, hung
on a cross, then stoned and shot
with arrows, the arrows and stones

miraculously, supposedly, bounced
back, striking their executioners,
they were then beheaded, three
younger brothers, inseparable in life,
shared their martyrdom, veneration
of the saints, churches, and relics, spread

quickly, popes and emperors adored
them, both Roman and Orthodox,

but confusion arose when bones
were circulated, a cathedral in Bremen
and a convent in Madrid both have
shrines revering their skulls, both
sets deemed powerful irresistible
healing agents, the Bremen shrine
were later moved to Munich, but

the skulls remained, in art the twins
are always together, one holding
a urine bottle, the other a medicine
box, but, apocryphally, they were
nearly separated in death, before
their martyrdom a grateful patient
forced Damian to accept three eggs,

Cosmas outraged by his brother's
weakness, by such worldly frailty,
demanded to be buried alone, apart
from his twin, their faithful followers
were about to comply when a camel,
speaking their language, trotted over
and begged them to bury the twins together.

Diogenes the Dog-Like

Known only by stories, the anecdotes
of those who knew, or heard of him,
Diogenes wrote ten books, seven
tragedies, and a volume of letters,
but all are lost, only the stories

survive, the most storied—Diogenes
wandering about Athens carrying
a lantern during daylight, when asked,
"I am looking for an honest man," he
found only deceivers and dissemblers,

a doctor to souls, Diogenes disdained
customs and values, vanity and folly,
wealth and chattel, the opinions
of others, forms, fashions and families,
society and politics, as all pretense,

he rejected all theology and beliefs
in the beyond, made a virtue of poverty
and preached the simplicity of nature,
happiness is independence, notorious
for stunts, he lived in the marketplace,

in a large tub, begged for a living,
and railed against decency, he ate
and slept wherever, whenever, he
defecated in a theater, urinated
on people, and masturbated in public,

"If only it were as easy to banish hunger
by rubbing my belly," indifferent to
class and power, reputation and rank,
he taunted Alexander the Great, who
wanted to meet the eccentric philosopher,

who found him in the marketplace sorting
through human bones, when asked why
he replied, "I am searching for the bones
of your father but cannot distinguish them
from those of a slave," Diogenes disrupted

lectures, scorned Plato, eating noisily,
mocking people for pretensions
to wisdom, he advocated asceticism,
a life not acquiring, but disposing,
the stupidity of property and luxury,

he is credited with coining the word
"cosmopolitan," proclaiming "I am
a citizen of the world," without loyalty
to place, a radical statement when
identity converged with city-state,

he founded the school of dogs, for he
admired their honesty, their lack
of guile, shame, deceit, or sham,
their bodily functions in public,
their ability to guard and protect,

their capacity to distinguish friends
from foes, the term "cynic" derives

from a Greek word for "dog-like," he is
known for his dog-like conduct, for being
one of the world's greatest cynics.

The Cross and Red Rose

Grafting cross and red rose, Rosicrucians seek higher
knowledge, esoteric erudition hidden from humanity
unprepared to receive it, secret followers with secret
understanding, passed down by few for centuries,
concealed arcane alchemies for transmuting people
rather than gold, the Universal Reformation of Mankind,
mystic Christians of the occult, the Rosicrucian furor

erupted in early seventeenth century Germany,
paralleling the Thirty Years' War, when millions
died, three manifestoes revealed the existence
of a secret magical society of philosopher doctors
who were at work to save humanity, the College
of Invisibles, promising to teach the nine stages
of the threefold, body, soul, spirit, rousing human

consciousness, developing Mastery of Life, connection
with the miraculous, a thoughtful life well lived,
the mysteries of life revealed, the illusions of time
and space dissolved, Egyptian mysteries purified
by the higher teachings of Christ, east and west,
past and present, actuality and reality, all merged,
Ormus a Gnostic sage, converted by Mark, created

the Order, the concealed knowledge rediscovered
by Christian Rosenkreuz, a man who never was,
whose family was put to death, witches and heretics,
who, a five-year-old boy, was saved by another

heretic, an Albigensian monk, later, while traveling
in the East, Rosenkreuz uncovered upon the mysteries,
and initiated eight doctors, sworn bachelors sworn

to secrecy, illuminati before the illumination, who
carried the burden, the hidden wisdom, passed
down in secret schools where knowledge was
disguised for better times, mystical libraries without
access, Rosenkreuz published the manifestoes,
supposedly, causing the furor, the promise
of a better world offered during violent tumult,

but the bloody patriarchs, fighting for their own
truths, dissented, and Rosicrucians, so hopeful,
 were hunted as heretics, yet still the promise of light
in darkness, of a better world, lingers, and some,
yearning for higher knowledge, the secrets of life,
find their way to AMORC, The Ancient Mystical
Order Rosae Crucis has local chapters near you.

Things Once Thought to Have Magical Power, and Perhaps Still Do

Rabbit's feet, bear claws, swallow stones,
cowrie shells, mandrake root, sassafras root,
tobacco, bird nests, elder, blackthorn,
datura, hemlock, wormwood, hellebore,
henbane, larkspur, patchouli, basil, rosemary,
apple blossoms, peaches, absinth, chamomile,
lavender, yarrow stalks, valerian, Psilocybin
mushrooms, coca plants, wine, beer, rum,
shoes, bottles, bottle trees, witch bottles,
witch balls, dolls, puppets, worry dolls,
urine cakes, maize, tea leaves, magnets,
compasses, the elusive Philosopher's Stone,
 the Eye of Horus, roses, crosses, rose crosses,
Ouija boards, scrying mirrors, wands, dowsing
rods, antlers, porcupine quills, cloaks, vests,
robes, hats, helmets, arrows, birds, lightning,
thunder, storms, crystals, crystal balls, gems,
precious stones, magic stones, stone tablets,
fairy stones, rune stones, runes, rocks, cymbals,
drums, horns, trumpets, songs, music, water,
wells, springs, water falls, water bowls, bones,
carvings, fetishes, statues, altars, vaults,
temples, caves, tunnels, secret rooms, frogs,
scorpions, unicorns, buffalo, bears, scarabs,
dice, astrodice, Magna Mater, Venus, Madonna,
Ganesh, saints, petroglyphs, scrolls, paintings,
icons, charms, amulets, brooches, rings, bracelets,
necklaces, medallions, pendants, magic boxes,
sator squares, tarot cards, cards, lanterns, chakras,
mantras, obelisks, arches, architecture, cauldrons,

brooms, bells, chalices, pentacles, triangles, candles,
candelabras, incense, incense burners, daggers,
spears, ogham staves, swords, talismans, idols,
cameras, photographs, hypnosis, stars, barn stars,
the zodiac, angels, demons, dragons, spells,
incantations, codes, seals, symbols, grimoires,
masks, numbers, inscriptions, curses, rituals,
costumes, wheels of fortune, the Hamsa,
hagodays, letters, words, alphabets, languages,
texts, almanacs, rocks, mountains, the Tree of Life,
trees, wind, dust devils, smoke, fire, will o' the wisp,
potions, blood, blood lettings, sacrifices, poisons,
wu ku, knots, weavings, blankets, dreams, trances,
dances, rosaries, animals, clouds, breath, touch, people.

The Black Death Was Not Black at First

The Black Death was not black at first,
not in the fourteenth century, not during
those few catastrophic years, from 1347
to 1353, when populations in Europe,
West Asia, the Middle East, and North
Africa were decimated, estimates vary,
70 million to 200 million died, villages
voided of populace in days, entire regions
ravaged, cities the worst death zones,
Paris losing half its population, as did
Hamburg, Bremen, and London, Florence
lost 80 percent of its population in only
4 months in 1348, the living unable to bury
the dead, rivers choked with corpses,
Europe never recovering its 1300 population
until 200 years later, The Black Death
was rather known as the great death, *magna
mortalitas*, the plague, the great pestilence,
God's vengeance, the end of the world,

When the Plague Arrived in Sienna, May 1348, a Found Poem

Father abandoned child, wife husband, one
brother another; for this illness seemed to strike
through breath and sight. And so they died,
and none could be found to bury the dead
for money or friendship. Members of a household
brought their dead to a ditch as best they could,
without priest, without divine offices . . . great
pits were dug and piled deep with the multitude
of dead. And they died by the hundreds both
day and night . . . And as soon as those ditches
were filled more were dug . . . And I, Agnolo di
Tura . . . buried my five children with my own
 hands. And there were also those who were
so sparsely covered with earth that the dogs
dragged them forth and devoured many bodies
throughout the city. There was no one who wept
for any death, for all awaited death. And so many
died that all believed it was the end of the world.

Why is the Devil a Black Man, Always?

Why is the devil a Black Man, always?
in thousands of references, in demonology
tracts scribbled by zealous monks, all white,
all attacking heresy, rebellion against God,
Christ the Prince of Light contending against
"the Power of Darkness," in countless sad
stories accusing women of witchcraft,

the accused, time and again, tortured
to confess, in intense agony, confessing
to stop the torment, confessing they consorted
with a Black Man, signing his book, dancing
wildly at what, of course, Black Sabbaths,
offering fealty to their dark lord, the anal kiss,
infernal painful coupling, the devil's two-

pronged phallus, the Salem narratives, sunless
texts, offer scores of examples, the devil
"appearing ordinarily as a small Black man,"
witchcraft the "Work of Darkness," "a dark
subject," "the devil improves the Darkness,"
"Dark things now in America," "in the shape
of a Black Man," "the Black Man whispered

to her," "she did ride by the Meeting house,
behind the Black Man," "by the assistance
of the Black Man," "the giant Black Man came
to her," "She looks upon a black man," "the Black
Man (as the witches call the Devil)," "a black thing
with a blue Cap," blackness ever iniquitous,
yes, of course, antithetical polarities, sightless

oppositions of light and dark, good and evil,
godly and pagan, celestial radiance preordained
to crush the black hand, wickedness void of
divine illumination, an omnipotent God allowing
the Prince of Darkness, humanity's scourge, those
early Christians, fervent believers, comprehending
only dualisms, a simplistic schematic to explain

the inexplicable, to account for misery, the Great
Chain of Being, white on top, black the bottom,
God created differences, high and low, fortune
and misfortune, and humans needed distinctions,
the othering of the alien, us and them, yet a bigotry
virulent and venomous, misperceiving a world
split into black and white, without any gray.

Tituba

She appeared and disappeared, and nothing
survives, before or after the hysteria, her life
a mystery, her body property bought and sold,
owned by others, recorded as an "Indian,"
as was her husband "John," Parris purchased
her in Barbados before he/they left for Boston
in 1680, his sugar plantation failing, selling off

what he could, taking little but chattel, she might
have been young, a teenager in a new world, a cold
climate, a slave subservient to whims and demands,
owned by a feckless, self-righteous master, quick
to feel piqued, prone to self-pity, she a nothing
in this new world order, a servant serving another's
family, suspected of deviltry, Parris had married soon

after arriving, marrying the most beautiful woman
in Salem Village, the union producing three children,
Betty the middle child, nine years-old when the storm
erupted, her cousin Abigail eleven, both vulnerable
to fear, illness, anxiety, Puritan foreboding, both
close to her, and she to them, their daily constant
interactions, the beautiful mother often bed-ridden,

perhaps she told them about the Venus Glass, the egg
white in water that became, not a prince, but a coffin,
terrifying the girls, the burden of conversion affliction,
then the fits began, spasms and screams, jerking
and lurching, hiding under furniture, crying, barking,
shrieking of unnatural torments, she was an easy
target once Dr. Griggs diagnosed "the evil hand,"

suspicion rampant, who's the witch, she tried
to help, baking the witch cake, an occult skill,
the cake meal mixed with the girls' urine, fed
to a dog, Parris beat her for the cake, then beat
her to confess, the first confession, her words
shattering the village, inciting the contagion,
the accusations, the girls had turned on her,

naming her, the beggar woman, the fallen woman,
all three carried off in chains, her words taken
by Corwin, one of the judges, she said she saw
a thing like a man who told her to serve him,
who threatened to hurt her if she did not hurt
the girls, the devil's emissaries, a hog, a great black
dog, two cats, one red, another black, as big as

a little dog, and a little yellow bird, the Black Man
promising her the yellow bird and pretty things
if she would sign the book and serve him, she
said she saw the yellow bird suck on the beggar
woman's right hand, she said she saw things she
could not name, one of them had wings, two legs,
and a head like a woman, another a thing all hairy

all over with two legs that walked upright but
only two or three foot high, the creatures
and imps tormenting her, forcing her to join
them, to hurt the children, finally she marked
the book, a pin tied to a stick, the ink red like
blood, after the dark winter, the summer's
hangings, she recanted in the fall, but no

one cared, everyone knew Indians worshipped
the devil, she languished in jail, Parris refusing
to pay her jail fees, in the spring, a full year after
the frenzy, an unknown person paid her fees
and took her away, never heard or mentioned
again, leaving only the lurid details the judges
pressed from her, Tituba, Salem's central figure.

Martha Carrier, Queen of Hell

When she was carried to the gallows,
Martha Carrier was either forty-two or
forty-nine, records are inexact, Salem
villagers lined the streets as her cart
passed, watching, some jeering, all
spellbound by the King of Terrors, by
a condemned witch departing for hell;

after she was launched into eternity
her broken body was dragged by its
halter to a common grave between
two rocks, barely two feet deep, with
two others put down in the war against
the Devil's horde. Astride a horse, Cotton
Mather, unflinching, watched her hang,

never doubting she had taken unholy
sacrament and signed the Book, a soul past
hope, traded away for paltry pleasures;
later, to proclaim his righteousness, his
sacred duty, and quell the creep of doubt,
the gnarl of critics, Mather marked her,
the clearest proofs of testimony, of spectral

evidence, clearly a rampant hag, an ungodly
mother, the queen of hell; carefully, he
catalogued the testimony of her accusers,
the Meeting House her theater of absurd,
her ungracious court, where the Salem girls,
 unrestrained, performed their bewitchment,
their wild histrionics, where words buried

Word, where hysteria condemned, a furious
frenzy, thrashing, twisting, shrieking accusations,
"it was Martha Carrier, or her Shape, that grievously
Tormented them, by Biting, Pricking, Pinching,
And Choaking"; helplessly, the magistrates
and ministers, grave men of grim authority,
watched the devil's power, when fearing

the girls could not survive their bedlam, they
ordered Carrier tightly bound, which eased
the pandemonium; defiant, she scorned
her accusers, when the girls complained
of "having their Necks twisted . . . by the Shape
of this Carrier," she declared, "Its no matter
though their Necks had been twisted quite off,"

when the girls cried out they saw the ghosts
of the thirteen Andover smallpox victims hovering
over the court, she accused her accusers, "It is false
 and a shame for you to mind what these say,
 that are out of their wits"; guilty before verdict, she
listened as neighbors indicted neighbor, a litany
of "extraordinary and unaccountable Calamities,"

Benjamin Abbot, who argued with her over land,
declared, after she cursed him, he was plagued
with sores which oozed "Gallons of Corruption,"
Allin Toothaker, who fought with her son, testified
he "fell down flat . . . and had no power to stir" until
"the shape of Martha Carrier got off his breast," two
other neighbors asserted that "this malicious Carrier . . .

strangely bewitched" their cattle, three confessed
witches, to save themselves, claimed Carrier carried
them to witch meetings, "enticing them into the snare
of the Devil," compelling them to partake in "Diabolical
sacrament," the "Bread and Wine" of damnation,
the most damning testimony, Carrier's 18-year-old
son and 7-year-old daughter, confessed joining

the devil's legions at their mother's direction, though
John Proctor, himself among the accused and destined
for the gallows, swore the children were tortured
to confess, to accuse their mother; she had no
chance, a scapegoat, soon a name mentioned
whenever a new person was accused; in 1711,
to atone for its sins, Massachusetts apologized

to Carrier's husband for hanging his wife, awarding
a small compensation, 7 pounds and 6 shillings; ever
righteous, never wavering, forever believing good was
at war with evil, Mather, in his final "Memorandum,"
swore "the Devil had promised her, that she should be
Queen of Heb," sovereign queen of all cursed souls
damned to burn for all eternity in everlasting hell fire.

Giles Corey, A Gruesome Death

Peine forte et dure (Law French for "hard and forceful punishment") was a method of torture formerly used in the common law legal system, in which a defendant who refused to plead ("stood mute") would be subjected to having heavier and heavier stones placed upon his or her chest until a plea was entered, or they died.

Caught up in the hysteria, the frenzied accusations,
legions of devils let loose, Giles Corey, eighty-one-
years old, was arrested, April 18, 1692, accused
by the accused, "a dreadful wizard" who afflicted
and tortured, demonic depravity, forcing innocent
girls into hell's dominion, yet refusing to plead he
 could not be tried, and protected his property
from forfeiture, and for standing mute in court,
was taken, stripped, and laid down in a vacant field
by Salem jail, to suffer peine forte et dure, the hard
and forceful punishment, crushed till he died or pled,
tortured for three days, without sustenance save
three morsels of the worst bread, three draughts
of standing water, heavier and heavier rocks placed
on boards over his chest, Sheriff Corwin, the weight
of authority, stood on the stones, one witness later
testified, "In the pressing, Giles Corey's tongue was
pressed out of his mouth; the sheriff, with his cane,
forced it in again," on the third day, beseeched to plea,
yet still refusing to plead, he died, accounts differ
on his last words, "more weight" or "more rocks" most
commonly recalled, also an imprecation, the antithesis
to confession, "Damn you, I curse you and Salem."

The Invisible World, Perceiving the Imperceptible

"We are winning the fight against an invisible enemy."
    —Vice President Mike Pence

The title says it all, Mather's *The Wonders*
of the Invisible World, his righteous defense,
of unrighteous trials, the wild histrionics,
the girls thrashing, jerking, pointing fingers,
the testimony of hostile neighbors, children
accusing parents, the paradox of pleas, perverse
inversions of confession, damnation redeems
while innocence condemns, convicted by
belief, by spectral evidence, by testimony
of apparitions, unseen and evil, shadows flitting
 about, beating, torturing, urging villagers
to sign the Book, a fiendish plague unleashed,
 devils and witches swarming, assailing,
assaulting the upright most grievously, shape-
shifting specters witnessed and accused,
indicted for inflicting grievous suffering,
the horrid courts, the nineteen executions,
ministers and magistrates alike perceiving
the imperceptible, the invisible world.

Sorcery, Seduction, and Dame Alice

An uncommon woman, appearing and disappearing
in the early fourteenth century, the first woman
accused of acquiring magical powers by having sex
 with a demon, the first woman tried for witchcraft
as a heretic, the first woman in Ireland condemned
for witchcraft, whose case caused a decade's long
battle between secular and sacred powers, who

became the Bishop of Ossory's personal crusade,
to damn her, to advance Church's sovereignty,
Alice Kyteler married four times, and each time
acquiring her husband's wealth and property,
her stepchildren, aghast, outraged at penurious
 inheritance, accused her of maleficium, of using
sorcery to seduce their fathers, beguiling them

of their riches, of emasculating them, accusing
her in the Bishop's ecclesiastical court, the Bishop,
ambitious to prove his zeal, anxious to wield
inquisitional license, the tearing of flesh to confess,
declared his Kilkenny diocese a hotbed of devil
worshippers, and launched his holy war, assailing
the devil and all demons, Dame Alice, and all civil

rule that obstructed his hallowed quest, aroused
with righteous fire, he excommunicated Alice,
then condemned her, on seven charges, that she
denied Christ and the Church, that she chopped up
three cocks, scattering their pieces at a crossroads,
 an offering to her demon lover, Robert, son of Art,
or Artisson, to gain her devilry, that she stole

the church keys and held black sabbaths at night,
casting spells, enchanting, vile maledictions
to corrupt Christians and subvert the Church,
that in the skull of a robber, she prepared a witch's
brew, the intestines and organs of cocks, worms,
fingernail clippings trimmed from the dead, and hair
from the buttocks of boys who died before baptism,

that she had intercourse with her incubus, Robert,
who appeared as a cat, a shaggy black dog, and a black
man, an ethiopis, fiendish carnal knowledge to obtain
wealth and power, that she used sorcery to murder
husbands and besot others with sordid lust to snatch
their substance and impoverish their stepchildren,
Alice disappeared, first to Dublin, then perhaps London,

yet the Bishop vented his inflamed passion on Petronella,
her maidservant, torturing her to confess she witnessed
execrable abominations, her lady's malefic sacrifices
to summon Robert from the depths of hell, that horrid
witch's brew, that once by daylight she watched her lady
have intercourse with her demon lover, that after they
were sated she used sheets from her own bed to wipe

clean the disgusting place, in return for her damning
testimony, the Bishop had Petronella whipped seven
times and then, on November 3, 1324, had her burned
at the stake, a kindness to prepare her for hell's eternal
flames, for decades the Bishop crusaded, ever at war
with those that opposed him, today in Kilkenny the Kyteler
Inn seduces with pints, and with a statue of Alice in front.

Purveyors of Horror

Purveyors of horror, those early terrorists,
evoked aberrant shapes and deviant
conditions, perverse realms of evil,
haunted houses furnished with darkness,
secrets, vermin, wraiths, and specters,
heartless fiends curding the light, avenging
unknown slights, tormenting helpless
women chained in shadows, malignant
brutes taking pleasure on pain, shrieks,
and howls, the destruction of innocence,
the strains of weeping, a ghoulish chorus,

these creators of chaos defied order
and reason, immersing all in murk, mist,
and gloom, devising savage scenes
stocked with iniquity and depravity,
animating what most is feared, merely
to shock, titillate, and propagate, packing
unspeakable cravings, exploiting terror for
dollars, these early terrorists of the bazaar,
 these Gothic writers, fed strange hungers,
a commerce of cobwebs, dismal dens,
hidden passageways, hopeless groans,
and heartless demons as leisure reading.

Chimeras, Our Monsters

More than just make believe, our monsters
are quite real, living in darkest visions, in
the impulsive id that imagines things going
bump in the night, imagining the unspeakable
that becomes spoken, things feeding on
children, ripping apart virgins, pouncing on
helpless victims, martyrs of human horror,
their gaze kills, their breath incinerates,
their venom destroys, their hunger for
shredding human flesh and bone insatiable,
their desire for blood unquenchable,
the worst deaths imaginable, everyone
has one, or several, and their clawing,
crunching, gnashing, and tearing, their
vileness and malevolence, their relentless
cravings, all tell true tales of terror, all facts
of fiction, of the sudden frights and dismal
dread of what's felt but never perceived
outside dusk and shadows, our poor monsters.

Take for example, the chimera, an ugly and
deadly beast, a mad amalgam of several
beasts, the ravenous head of a female lion
with pendulous breasts, a most disagreeable,
fire-breathing goat rising from the spine,
and for a tail a venomous serpent incessantly
hissing and seething with implacable rage. What
nightmare and narrative framed this monster,
progeny of a murderous giant and a creature
half woman and half snake, sibling to Cerberus,
Hydra, and Sphinx? Monstrous and merciless,

a terrible temper, ransacking and destroying,
what dark fear conjured this creature into
being, what need was there for such terror?
for thousands of years the chimera roamed
and ravaged freely until no longer needed,
until the imagination conceived new monsters.

New World Wonders

The New World astounded the Old
with marvels and miracles, wonders
of boundless possibilities, as those
who first journeyed reported rarities
incomparable, igniting imaginations,
Oviedo, who perhaps penned the first
literary work in the New World, described

"spiders of a marveylous biggenesse, her
bodye as bygge as a sparrow. Vypers leape
in the ayre to assayle men. Adders so redde
that in the night they appear like burnynge
coals. Byrdes so little that the whole body
is no bigger than the toppe of the biggest
finger of a man's hand. Many toades so big

that the bones of sum of them appear
to bee the bones of cattes." A contemporary,
but no friend, Las Casas denounced Oviedo
as "one of the greatest tyrants, thieves,
and destroyers of the West Indies, whose
Historia contains almost as many lies as
pages," yet Oviedo gave the Old World
strange fruit, the pineapple, and a strange

bed, the hammock, and described a strange
practice of cooking meat over a smoldering
smoldering fire, which the natives called
barbacoa, he was also one of the earliest
to describe a most miraculous medicinal plant,
tobacco, which among its many uses was
thought to cure headaches, kidney stones,

blisters, toothaches, and bad breath, so
fashionable it became that soon English
schoolboys at Eton were instructed how
to properly smoke their pipes, inhaling,
were required to carry pipe and tobacco
in their school bags, and whipped if they
did not habitually smoke their pipes.

The Alternate Facts of the New World, Fictions as Truth

Writing well consists of thinking, feeling and expressing well, of clarity of mind, soul and taste . . . The style is the man himself.
   —Georges-Louis Leclerc, Comte de Buffon

Omniscient and ignorant, Buffon believed
the New World inferior compared to the old,
assertive, imperious, his self-confidence
unassailable, yet abysmally insensible of his
incomprehension, Buffon pronounced a land
he never saw as degenerate, its animals,
plants, natives, and climate all undeveloped,

corrupted forms of Old World manifestations,
mostly "a frigid mass," and "thinly inhabited,"
where Nature was "always rude, and sometimes
deformed," where "air and earth overloaded
with humid and noxious vapors are unable
to purify themselves," where only "reptiles
and insects" proliferate, where only "cold

men and feeble animals" can endure, all life
is shrunken, misshapen under "a niggardly sky
and unprolific land," "the animals of America
are tractable and timid, very few ferocious
and none formidable," as for the natives,
"Nature treated them like a stepmother.
The organs of generation are small and feeble.

They have no body hair and no ardor for
the female." His grand theory, the cruel
stepmother withheld the "basic molecules
of life" until late in creation, after Europe

and Asia, with little left to give America,
except fetid swamps and impenetrable
forests, dreadful, wretched, deficient life.

Though thought to be the greatest expert
on the Americas, Corneille de Pauw was
far worse, having never visited the land he
reviled, and rejecting the observations
of those who did, he intoned everything
in the New World was inferior due to poor
climate and dismal land, especially pitiful

were the people, "The American, strictly
speaking, is neither virtuous nor vicious,"
"the timidity of his soul, the weakness of his
intellects, the necessity of providing for his
subsistence, the powers of superstition,
the influence of climate, all lead him far
wide of the possibility of his improvement;

but he perceives it not; his happiness is,
not to think, to remain in perfect inaction;
to sleep a great deal; to wish for nothing,
when his hunger is appeased; and to be
concerned about nothing but the means
of procuring food when hunger torments
him . . . In his understanding there is no

gradation, he continues an infant to the last
hour of his life." "The Europeans who pass
into America degenerate, as do animals;
a proof that the climate is unfavourable
to the improvement of either man or animal."
"This degradation of humanity must be
imputed to the vitiated qualities of the air

stagnated in their immense forests, and
corrupted by noxious vapours from standing
waters and uncultivated grounds." Native
Americans can barely speak: "There are none
of these languages in which it is possible
to count above three . . . they lack a sufficient
number of terms capable of enunciating

general concepts." Such degenerate life, dogs
lost their bark and contracted syphilis, the only
creatures larger than those of Europe were
"monstrous insects which grew to prodigious
size and multiplied beyond imagining." The Inuit
are "the most diminutive race of human kind"
yet "have enormous heads, are extremely fat

and corpulent, and much under-limbed," while
in the Caribbean exist "a sort of savages who have
hardly any neck, and whose shoulders rise
as high as the ears . . . These monsters appear,
at a certain distance, to have the mouth in
the middle of the breast . . . men without
heads." De Pauw, whose family later named

a university, concluded men of the New World
were so lacking in virility that they had milk
in their breasts. Jefferson, Franklin, Paine, Adams
all attacked the distortions, the untruths, yet
slanders continued well past the Enlightenment,
Europeans preferring to believe their alternate
facts, even when presented with evidence.

Divining Millerites

Once famous, then forgotten, the Millerites, fervent
believers, believed that the world was about to end,
that the Second Coming was occurring, that Christ
would embrace them, the virgins, in divine union,
and ascend to heaven, shutting the gates, stranding
the damned, a cleansing by fire; after years of cryptic
exegesis, William Miller, burnt over and reawakened,

predicted the Advent, exhorted his followers
to prepare, over five million Millerite publications,
Signs of the Times, hundreds of tent revivals, and
over a million followed, days were augured, usually
a spring date, sometime between 1843 and 1844,
people prepared, selling, giving away, disconnecting,
forsaking lives, eager and expectant, ready to meet

their end, waiting for ascension, for portended
bliss, heavenly wedlock, some donned white robes,
gathered on hilltops, when spring passed, merely
a slight miscalculation, October 22 was selected,
yet that day passed and the world endured,
causing the Great Disappointment, bewildered
believers, yearning for celestial caress, yet some

so devout they waited, day by day, each morning
flush with hope, the gates never closing, some
rejoined old congregations, old lives, while some
 became Shakers, believing Christ had already come,
now a Mother, schisms and sect building occurred,
Seventh-Day Adventists anxiously await, but Miller,
so devout, survived his prophecies by only a few years.

The Great Hanging, Gainesville, Texas, October 1862

Not so great, The Great Hanging,
forty-one were lynched, a few more
shot, around thirty were condemned
by a "Citizens' Court," which made
up its own rules, had no legal status,
and cared little for evidence, fourteen
or more, were simply dragged from jail

by a mob and hanged without process
or pretense of justice, condemned by
rumor and rancor, neighbors murdering
neighbors in the midst of madness and war,
stricken by fear and panic, the contagion
of violence fatal, incurable insanity, partisan
lynchings in enmity and inhumanity for

 treason and insurrection, for being
 Unionists, for refusing to be conscripted
into the Confederate Army, for opposing
the Sequestration Act that seized and sold
the property of "alien enemies," for signing
a petition objecting to exempting large
slaveholders from the draft, for resisting

the frenzy; ready for a fight, needing foes,
two Confederate officers created the court,
promoted the pandemonium, slaveowners
who together owned a quarter of all Cooke
County slaves, who appointed slaveowners
as jurors, although few residents owned slaves,
only eleven percent, and although at first few

wanted war, in 1859 seventy-three percent
voted for Sam Houston, a Unionist, in February
1861 sixty-one percent voted not to secede,
out of one hundred and twenty-two Texan
counties, Cooke was only one of eighteen
to vote for the Union, in March Texas seceded,
and the governor "deposed" for refusing

to take the pledge; in October 1862, rumors
rampant, the two slaveholders, infected
with righteous fever, began arresting citizenry
suspected of Union sympathies, of colluding
and conspiring, of subverting the Confederacy,
of being secret abolitionists, of being different,
one-hundred and fifty taken up in thirteen

days, ultimately more than two hundred,
at first only one or two were hanged,
then handfuls strung up as hysteria spiraled,
the fourteen lynched without trial could not
slake the thirst as mobs gathered, and nineteen
who were acquitted were re-arrested and
 hanged, without new evidence, the tainted

breeze lasted for weeks, Governor Lubbock
praised the hangings, but President Davis was
shocked, and generals were replaced, while
Northern papers expressed outrage, Frank
Leslie's Illustrated Newspaper featured a garish
engraving, dozens of dangling bodies, as people
picnicked nearby, refusing to recognize the rot;

a century later people still refused to look up,
in 1964, as the Beatles arrived, as race riots ignited,
as the Civil Rights Act became law, the Texas
Historical Commission erected a commemorative
marker, defending the hangings, claiming the forty-
one men deserved their fate, all having "sworn
to destroy their government, kill their leaders,

and bring in Federal troops," nonsense stirred
up by the summer's heat, in 2012 an anniversary
commemoration was scrapped—bad press, but
the Sons of Confederate Veterans created a video
portraying the victims as "traitors" justly executed
for passing information to the enemy, finally, in
2014, a privately-funded memorial listed the names.

The Rigor of Phrenology, a Pseudoscience

A science that wasn't, that caused a frenzy
of head tapping and cranial measuring lasting
decades, that launched thousands of pamphlets,
books, journals, and societies, phrenology
propounded the connection between cranium
and character, between external physiognomy
and internal personality, at worst between skull

and skulduggery, here was a science that wasn't,
that divined the heart's secrets by mapping
the skull's topography, a geography of peaks
and valleys that revealed inner propensities,
size mattered, the greater the bump or lump,
the greater the propensity, with methodological
rigor phrenologists used fingertips to expose

what could not be seen, to feel what could not
be disclosed, the brain a mash-up of twenty-
seven organs, or more, each organ a separate
faculty that determined personality, that shaped
 identity, the bump at the back of the skull,
for example, controlled philoprogenitiveness,
the sex organ, closely encircled by amativeness,

adhesiveness, and combativeness, yet the rigor,
at best, was doubtful, believing their scientific
validity, and using illustrated porcelain heads,
maps, and charts, self-perpetuating head-tapping
to expound the mind's mysteries, phrenologists
predicted the predictable, white males declaiming
that the Caucasoid race the most beautiful, the most

advanced, that female brains were undeveloped
for success in the arts and sciences, but whose
organs were larger for childcare and religion,
that lower orders could be ranked from least
to most evolved, that some at the lower end,
people supposed as aboriginal, lacked cerebral
organs for complicated reasoning, for higher

learning, trusting their creed, their gospel,
those touching heads believed their science
exposed enigmas of peculiarity, illuminated
darkness, uncovered the work of God, only
the scams of grafters, quacks with cartoonish
schematics, curtailed the craze, yet doctrines,
once believed, linger long after the belief.

Monroe Edwards, The Forger Who Could Not Spell

A forger and fraud, a swindler and scammer,
Monroe Edwards died in Sing Sing, muttering,
delusional, consumptive, in life a handsome
man, well-dressed, he's mentioned in Bartleby,
both adept scriveners driven beyond the edge
by excessive copying, by extreme withdrawals,
both spent time in the Tombs, wanting a touch

of realism in his unreal story, Melville used
the name, then infamous, the Great Forger,
there had been a sensational trial for a series
of fraudulent letters and false signatures,
from New Orleans cotton brokers to New York
bankers, securing huge loans for non-existent
cotton, upwards of fifty thousand dollars,

to shield himself, Edwards sent a forged letter
to the police accusing another man, but he
was arrested and forty-four thousand dollars
were found in his room, he forged letters
and checks to hire six lawyers, including both
a senator and a representative, but he was
convicted, a bank teller identified him, his

elegant appearance, a bank bag was found
in his possession, and the capstone, the same
misspellings were found in his papers and
his forged letters, resulting in a ten-year
sentence, the *New York Herald* published
the trial's proceedings, fifty-thousand copies,

the *National Police Gazette* soon published
*The Life and Adventures of the Accomplished
Forger and Swindler*, mingling fact and fiction,
adding a tragic romantic love story, a slave

who loved a swindler, a notorious confidence
man, there were as well several other accounts,
he began his corrupt career as a slaver, buying
indentured Blacks in Cuba and selling them
as slaves in Brazil and Texas, using his proceeds
to buy land in Brazoria County, a plantation he
named Chenango, also a slave market on Galveston

Bay, always grabbing, grasping, he defrauded
his partner, who sued, and who was awarded
$89,000, Edwards fled the Republic of Texas
for the United States, where he went north
to fleece abolitionists with stories of liberating
slaves in Texas, when pursued with questions
he sailed to England with the same scam,

but the Republic's London ambassador warned
to be wary of his schemes, and letters arrived
from singed abolitionists, ruining his business,
Edwards then launched his final swindle, at first
a huge success, a trunk full of money, but his
forgeries undid him, and even his lawyers,
hired with fake letters, never got paid.

Rules of Conduct, From an 1876 College Catalogue, a Found Poem

It is presumable that every student will have
some knowledge of the first principles of morality,
propriety, and decorum, and that it will therefore
be unnecessary to prescribe a complete code
 of specific rules and regulations. But it will be
expected and required of all students: 1. That

they be diligent in their study, punctual in their
attendance upon worship, recitation, examinations
and all other college exercises, and that they
promptly render a valid and satisfactory reason
to the proper officers for any delinquency. 2. That

they treat all persons, and especially the students
and teachers of the college, with becoming respect.
3. That they do not trespass upon the premises
of any person, and they in no way deface or injure
the property of the college. 4. That they attend

no exhibition of immoral tendency; no race course,
theatre, circus, billiard-saloon, bar room, or tippling
house. 5. That they neither introduce upon the premises
of the college, nor use there or elsewhere, any kind
of intoxicating beverage; and that they abstain from
the use of tobacco in the buildings of the college.

6. That they neither keep in their possession nor use
any firearms, a dirk, a bowie-knife, nor any other kind
of deadly weapon. 7. That they abstain from profanity,

the desecration of the Lord's day, all kinds of gaming
for a reward or prize of any kind, and from card playing

even for amusement; and also whatever else is
inconsistent with good order, good taste, and good
morals. 8. That they attend public worship every
Lord's day. 9. That they do not leave the college
until regularly dismissed at the close of the session,
without special permission of the Faculty.

The X, Sorry Y'all Had to Wait

The store's long gone, but the memory
remains, an old automotive and tire store
that sold bits of everything, located in
a shabby strip mall where there were dry
cleaning, barbecue, Chinese, loans, real
estate, insurance, and jewelry, everything
reasonably priced. The old man stood next
to the cash register, listening while a young
clerk read out the payment agreement,
 a formidable form, twenty-five dollars
a month forever for four tires, installed in
back. Stooped with the burden of years,
of decades living as a Black man in the Deep
South, of living a life inescapable, a life
restrained by race, a life defined by why,
by infectious lies, by the strangest fruit,
the old man nodded at each provision,
more patient than we were, until the clerk
handed him form and pen, still nodding, he
accepted, and, with meticulous care, marked his X,
blue ink on yellow paper, then straightening,
he turned to us in line, and spoke, a whispery
voice that echoes, "Sorry y'all had to wait."

The House Slaves, the Half Door

Six college kids kicked out of dorms,
looking for a summer house, more
interested in good times than grave
issues, awkward inquiries, yet in a small
town on the Eastern Shore, no one was
willing to rent, three unmarried
couples living in sin, one couple mixed,

an Asian boy, an Hispanic girl, we'd
go look at a rental only to learn,
with a brief smile and briefer story, "sorry,
it's just been rented," them wild pot-
smokin college kids, damn hippies,
we failed to perceive a world so unlike
our own, so we felt lucky the real estate

guy who rented to students had a farm
house out a ways from town, a sprawling
brick structure, rundown, abandoned for
decades, set high on a hill overlooking
a creek that flowed into the Bay,
a waterway for cotton and tobacco,
the house surrounded by open fields,

horse corn and soy beans now, a dozen
rooms with the broad main stairs blocked
off, we rented the downstairs, the kitchen
and one bathroom recently renovated,
outside half a dozen collapsed outbuildings,
out by the tree line a forlorn family plot
we knew was haunted, yet the strangest,

eeriest room a box above the kitchen, two
windows too high to reach, reachable only
by narrow, windowless stairs, the first
step so high we had to crawl like children,
climbing with hands and feet, the passage
dark and musty, a thin airless hall that led
to a half door, the door long gone, not even

chest high, we had to stoop low to enter,
we knew but didn't know, or care to know,
privileged college kids, a distant world too
close to comprehend, more concerned
with our pleasures, feeling righteous we
opposed the war, supported equal rights,
the revolution in the streets in our minds,

we had not read Douglass who grew up
nearby, who never knew his birth day,
nor recognized the past's intransigent
persistence, we were incapable of imagining
people who had to crawl up and bend over
to reach their beds, or realize they were
the lucky ones who lived in the big house.

A Student's Story

Abruptly, she walked in, "I'd like to talk
about my absences," and sat across
a glass-topped table, shuffling paper,
pens, and purse, looking out the window,
an exemplary student, straight As,
perfect GPA, but who had disappeared
for three weeks with no word, suddenly
reappearing, the same but not the same
 person, As and GPA discarded, careless
 work, attending a class, then absent
 the next. Coming to explain but unable
 to start, she sat waiting while pleasantries
were exchanged, then suddenly the burst,
"Last month I found out my mother was
really my grandmother, and I went searching
for my mother, but she had been killed
in a car accident last Christmas, down in
Laurel, she'd been drinking and lost control."

Words and sympathy all offered, profusely,
sincerely, and adjustments made, but what
solace, what commiseration, could there
ever be, a mother unknown, never to be
known, family destabilized by secrets, by
furtive motives, best she never knows?
Inevitably, secrets seep and ooze. She left
as quickly as she appeared, hurrying to get
somewhere. I never saw her again.

Aspiring to Higher Education, Or How a Chair Was Floored

Most were marvelous, the most hardworking,
reliable, and dedicated, living deferred lives,
yet a motley group with of dubious directions.
First, there was the TA who sat on the front table,
cross-legged, palms out, thumb and forefinger
circled, while chanting as the students wrote;
when asked what the hell, he replied: "I was
levitating to a higher realm," still humming when
he was escorted away. Then there was the TA
who accepted bribes from students, cash was
preferred, but he announced a preference, just
before Christmas and graduation, for single-malts,
aged at least fifteen years. There was one dear
sensitive soul who communed with trees, a tree
hugger literally, who asserted that trees conversed
with her, and who was found caressing a Live Oak
in the Grove, and who left abruptly for California.
And there was the righteous one who dropped
a Black student athlete's paper on the floor and who
then complained, fiercely, endlessly, that he did not
feel safe in his classroom after a chair was thrown
against a wall. There was, perhaps the most curious
and sad, the pretty SoCal girl, with a Stanford degree,
an alcoholic, who stopped wearing shoes, who wore
a dead goat for a coat, and who, come spring, began
to star in x-rated fraternity party porn films; students
complained about her dirty feet, but never her films.
The list runs on, all colorful, curious characters,
the ABD who claimed he had finished his degree
 and asked me to lie for him, several times, the ex-

Mormon cat killer who ran over a cat, intentionally,
the constantly sick and sallow vegan couple who lived
on potato chips, the vicious divorced woman whose
husband ran off with a Swedish girl, the endlessly
dissertating brother and sister who claimed, earnestly,
to have tenure, and the fragile woman who loved
being loved, who, left alone, slipped into nightmares,
believed the government was spying on her, and
covered her house with layers of aluminum foil.

The Human Space, The Human Condition

There's always this side and that,
near and far, here and there,
useful and useless, smart and stupid,
self and other, the me and the not
me, it's the gaps between us defines
us, lines drawn in sand, human space
leans towards edges and margins, borders
and boundaries, to constitute the human—
erase the lines, and we disappear.

In kindergarten, on the first day,
Roosevelt Pettijohn did not
want to be friends, his daddy
having told him not to mess
with white boys, to stick
with his own kind. When asked,
while on the playground swings,
side by side, he shoved away,
and ran off to his cousin, a safer
space, the swinging too dangerous.

Yet at the gates, when the beasts
are crouching, when dry winds scorch
the skies with dust clouds, roiling black
 brown masses swirling, darkening
horizons, there's always convergence,
the coming together, diverse
currents drawn together by greater
turbulence, the human condition
tends towards attachment, disparate
parts joining, little and late, yet linking.

In the second grade, we were drilled, small
scared children, having seen the poisonous
clouds, having heard the adults whisper, we
gathered in the basement hallway, pressed
against the cold tile of walls and floor, doing
whatever we were told to do, hunkering,
scrunching, covering, then Roosevelt leaned
over, his slender body shoved against mine,
"You playing ball after this?" Yes, yes, yes.

Reverend Cherry

Though a nice man, Reverend Cherry
got angry every Sunday, his face would
turn red, and his voice would get loud,
and he would yell at us, though I was
too young to know what he was yelling
about, or what people had done
to make him so angry, or why I had
to sit without squirming, I played
with his two sons, baseball mostly,
and suffered through piano lessons
with his wife, convinced that baseball
players never had to take piano lessons,
hearing without listening, daydreaming,
I always wondered if, in his black robe,
white collar, and red face, anyone else
thought he looked like a cherry.

Nicodemus The Cat

Nicodemus the cat, eighteen
years old, frail and infirm, does
little but howl, sleep, and eat,
a limp rag on the living room
floor, yet when picked up, and
cradled, he purrs contentedly,
when walked to the front windows,
tail twitching excitedly, he raises
his head, and watches his world.

Competition on Lake Worth and the West Fork

The bass fishing tournament got started
at first light, before I launched, thirty to
forty pickups and SUVs filling the parking
lot, spilling onto the grass, boat trailers
looking like the skeletal ribs of old wrecks,
still, the lake was glassy and calm, staying
out of the bass boat lanes, and pulling

close to shore, passed two disinterested
buzzards perched on the electrical tower,
its steeple relaying the grid to the far
shore, their black dots against a cloudless
morning sky, the photos turned out poorly,
paddled away from the open lake, passing
under the cement pillars of the highway

bridge, seeking the back channels that go
nowhere, rocked only by the wake of bass
boats zipping across the water to their
next secluded spot, the whine of outboards
buzzing like insects, I sought those spots
for myself, a deeper immersion, for clearer,
closer contact, a moment's transcendence,

I fished for photos, framing, adjusting,
yet lazily relied on auto modes, reliable
but sterile, the glint of sun reflected off
the water, dense colorations of green, blue,
and brown constantly shifting with cross-
currents of wind and river, the undirected
design of reed and marsh, the sycamores,

oaks, and mesquits rising above, leaning
over the water, hoping to capture shadows
mingled with light, the egrets and herons
before flight, and seeking forgiveness
from those I disturbed, while paddling
gently by those who conceded my
momentary presence, later I returned

with the stream of bass boats anxious
for the weigh-in, they let me slip by
and run ashore on a muddy strip near
the ramp, as I loaded and carried, one old
guy, sunburned and happy, mistaking me,
asked me how I did, "Just a lot of sun
and a few photos," he laughed and slapped

me on the back, a good joke unintended,
I heard the tournament director call out
the day's winners, those who hooked
the most, the biggest, the heaviest,
for fear of mercury, few will eat what
they caught, I left eager to get home, cool
off in the pool, and PhotoShop my catch.

On The Lee Side of Goat Island

On the lee side of Goat Island there's
a scene that can never be seen, but is,
a scattering of cotton clouds, a blue
sky, and calm water, so scenic cameras
fail, but across the island there's a steady
wind gusting over twenty, and the water's
rippled with chop and frothy white caps,
the paddle across open water was rough,
the constant thump of waves and spray,
and the push of crosscurrents, the kayak
pitching, tumbling, the paddle grabbing
air on the rises, but once committed
there's no turning back, to turn risks
overturning, keep heading into the wind,
keep pulling hard, deep long strokes
on the drops, taking the battering
to reach the calm water, Goat Island's
a crescent moon, a quarter mile of rock,
sand, scrub, raccoons, cranes, egrets,
even deer, a Monarch refuge of sunflowers
and milkweed, and trash from party people
camped for the day, and for those who
can read the water, there's always shelter.

The Goatman of Lake Worth

A story gave Goat Island its name, a wild
man, half man, half goat, seven feet tall,
matted in thick white fur, prone to violent
rage, in the summer of 69, on July 9, the story
was born, three young couples parked down
Shoreline Road near Greer Island, a secluded
spot where young people could be alone,

around midnight the beast dropped from a tree
and tried to grab a young woman, but the cars
sped off before it could drag her away, because
the witnesses were terrified, and a long gash
on one of the cars, the police investigated,
and newspapers reported, resulting in monster-
fever, truckloads of men with guns, beer, wine,

and whiskey headed out to hunt the creature,
followed by spectators equally loaded, the next
night dozens of people in a clearing known for
dumping witnessed the Goatman, on a high bluff
looking angry, throwing a tire 500 hundred feet,
making a plaintive, pitiful cry, everyone ran
away, including the deputies, five people claimed

they saw the monster snap off a thick oak branch
like a toothpick, another claimed it jumped on
the hood of his Mustang, causing him to crash,
the fever raged through summer and fall as stories
rambled on, and in November a man snapped
a grainy photo of the monster, a white, hairy thing
its back turned, moving away in tall grass, a Sasquatch

if there ever was one, though the photographer
thought it was probably a prank, stories live and
breathe, and books, articles, and documentaries
have been made about the Lake Worth Monster,
a local brewing company sold Goatman beer, lore
endures, and witnesses persist, and the Texas Bigfoot
Research Center and scores of cryotozoologists are

assured the Goatman lives on, though a persistent
rumor lingers, that early on the police captured
a small group, students from a local university, out
on the edges of the Trinity River's West Fork, one
dressed in a white ape costume, how brave, how wild,
how foolish they were, if they were, to give life
to the story during the monster-hunting frenzy of 1969.

Kayaking In Rough Currents

Rising and falling, a slim needle
pulled towards inexact directions,
the relentless rocking of sky
and horizon, the roll of wind
and water, the bow shakes
and shoulders strain to keep
a true course, defied by chop
and swell, a moment's rest
and momentum's lost, the kayak
pitches and lurches, its thin skin
of fiberglass and resin, at once
stable and unsteady, a precarious
balance, with little fathoming
of depths, yet fixed in intention,
the motion forward, the paddling
pulls into the froth, a steady
need to move ahead, getting
pushed back, turned around
and tilted down, is not an option,
better to head into the wind
and waves, a sheltered cove,
the chance of calm water around
the bend, that far point, impels
endless motion and venture.

Brazos des Dios

The Spaniards named it Arms of God, its embrace
cradles New Mexico and Texas, the gracious Brazos,
through the dry hills of scrub, pine, and mesquite,
the river startles winding its way through the green
hills, banded by gravel and sand, gray sandstone bluffs,
and steep banks of red clay, its watercolors touched
and dabbed constantly, the river chooses its own course,

a slow selection over eons, flow shaping way, moving
slowly, tumbling giant boulders and rocks along its path,
drifting at an eternal pace unimaginable, the river is
shared, abundant life, sandpipers, cormorants, herons
rise at human approach, while the martins dipping
and darting over mounds of shore grass ignore what
does not concern them, never silent, the river's a chorus,

shallows rippling over rocks, birds hidden in foliage calling
to one another, perhaps warblers passing through, their
journey long, the wind's constant, and at times deceives,
the flow moving towards a distant sea while strong breezes
drive the surface back, the gusts pushing the chop high
enough to crest, stopping the forward motion of kayaks
and canoes, below the Possum Kingdom dam there's

little to intrude, just the fences and signs, No Trespassing,
but the signs are shabby, paltry disruptions, and the river's
a public road up to the gradient boundaries, the stream
bed and lower banks cannot be fenced off, the arrogance,
the shamelessness of humans, the river's gravel shoals and sand
banks the work of ages, the steady crush and grind of history
beyond human comprehension, the water's meaningful,

each drop soaked with inconceivable passage, to paddle
the Brazos coalesces time and place, and humbles, human

life a quick spark in darkness, the tiniest grain of sand cast
on an endless beach, the ache of arms and shoulders teaches
the river's lesson, the glide of life, downstream there's
always new wonder around the unending bends, patiently
the river lectures, but still we fail to hear.

Of Gods and Planets, and a Free Lunch

In today's mail, The Neptune Society,
America's Most Respected Cremation
Services, offered me a free lunch,
at a local Outback steakhouse, and
an Informational Seminar, and if
I attend there's a Chance to WIN
A WEEKEND GETAWAY FOR TWO,
though direction, transportation,
and location were not indicated.

A glossy and colorful flyer, 8 by 11,
with a striking photo of two women
perhaps a mother and daughter, both
brilliantly smiling, touching heads,
and holding hands, the older woman
has wrinkles, gray hair, red lipstick,
and wears a blouse checked with tiny
triangles with tinier yellow triangles
inside, perhaps flames, and perhaps
she's preparing for her getaway to back
beyond, and is thanking her daughter
for helping with the dispensation of her
earthly remains, a tender moment
promoting the rendering of corpses,
ashes to ashes, a powerful symbol.

Google does not mention how the Society
got its name, whether a god or a planet, or
happenstance, but reveals its founding
in 1973, its Memorial Reef, 3.25 miles off
the coast of Key Biscayne, and its Columbarium,
a San Francisco landmark, suitable places
for venerating ashes, Google does mention
Walt Disney's great nephew tried to purchase

the company for $11.5 million, though the deal
fell apart, but does not say why, it concludes
with controversies, accusations of mishandling
money and bodies. Google does not gratify.

In myth, the skeletal remains of outworn
beliefs, Neptune is one of the greatest gods,
 one of the three brothers, lords of heaven,
earth, and underworld, who conquered Saturn,
their father, he ruled over all watery realms,
oceans, rivers, lakes, even natural springs,
and horses and horse-racing, not the nicest
Olympian, he was violent, bad-tempered,
unpredictable, greedy, and given to sudden
outbursts and vendettas, poor Ulysses, and like
many male gods a lustful immortal, fathering
children with his wife, or consort, Salacia,
a salacious female deity, goddess of salt water,
Triton and Proteus two of their progeny,
he even coupled with the unsightly Medusa,
a lecherous coupling producing Pegasus,
the winged horse, during the summer festivals
of Neptunalia, men and women mixed
without restraint, and bulls were sacrificed,
celebrations of fertility, a bearded muscular
god, he's depicted with a trident, the three-
pronged fisherman's spear, and usually rides
a chariot piloted either by dolphins or horses,
and is often surrounded by a retinue of sea
creatures and naked female nymphs.

First observed by telescope in 1846, the planet
Neptune, the furthest planet from the Sun (if
Pluto and other distant celestial bodies are
discounted) got its name because of its bluish
color, one of the ice giants, Neptune is the fourth

largest planet, the third most massive, and has
thirteen moons, an icy atmosphere of hydrogen,
helium, hydrocarbons, nitrogen, and methane,
which gives it its blue tinge, it's not an inviting
nor habitable planet, though one of its moons,
Triton, might one day support a space colony
according to one optimistic internet source.

Though appreciative of the Neptune's Society's
invitation, I decline, being incurious about
the benefits of pre-planning and indifferent
to the dispensation of my earthly remains, yet
I remain grateful for pausing to wonder why
the business was named after a disagreeable
God and an inhospitable planet, though my
wondering's neither exceptional nor discerning,
a moment's reflection reveals oceans always
have been linked with the eternal, the endless
rocking, the calm after storms, the ceaseless
tides, its horizon always beckoning to what's
beyond, ultimately, water gives life and takes life,
and in that space between, that frail duration,
we hunger for knowledge of gods and planets.

The Ten Worst Teachers

The Ten of the Worst Teachers Ever, with Photos

1. The middle school teacher who taped
her student's mouth shut, to keep
Jazlyn from talking, double layers of scotch
tape, and a third layer when she coughed.
2. The middle school teacher who published
an erotic novel featuring her students, graphic
teenage sex fantasies, she had them practice
orgasmic moaning in class. 3. The two middle
school teachers who performed a lap dance
during a basketball game halftime, two teachers,
one chair, way-too many gyrations and
simulations. 4. The primary school teacher
who told her seven-year-old students there
was no Santa. 5. The middle school teacher
who accidently sent copies of a self-made
sex tape home with her fifth graders, thinking
it was a school excursion, a candle-lit bath
and intimate touching. 6. The primary school
teacher who took photos of hair styles, then mocked
them on FaceBook, the Jolly Rancher braids,
the birthday candle braids. 7. The primary school
teacher who routinely sprayed her Bangladeshi
 students with air freshener, complaining they
smelled like curry and onions. 8. The middle
school teacher who repeatedly hit a special needs
student with a glue stick until his thumb bled.
9. The middle school teacher who got arrested
for drunken teaching, prescription pills
suspected, staggering in class corroborated.
and 10. The high school teacher who attached
McDonald's job application forms to failed math
exams, the big fat red Fs not enough to humiliate.

The worst teachers? Miserable, lamentable, deplorable,
and contemptible, yes, but worst no. Worse, perhaps
the quiet prevarications of hate, the tender execrations
of disdain, or perhaps worse than worse, the sluggish
indifference of negligence and arrogance, perhaps.

A Very Lost Cause

I declared war on a word,
a parasite, presumptuous,
pretentious, always inserting
itself where there's no need,
no purpose, no benefit,
it's everywhere, swarming,
seething, replicating, but
useless, always pretending
to strengthen as it weakens,
shaking their heads, pointing
at maps and screens, generals
bunched in war rooms were
very sorry, they could do little
to stem the tide, politicians,
nodded happily, felt my plight,
but were also very sorry,
they could do nothing, while
endlessly using the word,
a pretense of sincerity, a prop
of eminence, students adore
the word so much its use is
automatic, subconscious, their
paragraphs stippled with it,
though the syllabus, very
clearly, banishes the word.

Arkansas River at Dawn

The river runs towards boundless, rushing
over rocks worn smooth, immeasurable
years, silver glint flashes over and
around boulders, flashes of light
immemorial, while bluegreen water
swirls in deep pockets, scattered
around ancient red rocks, bright in early
light, and dippers and scissortail flycatchers
flit and dart about rocks and water,
brushed by glacial ages the river, human
echo distant, and fluttering in light breeze,
the grace of cottonwood forgives all for all.

Past Dalhart

Way out there somewhere, west past
Dalhart, there's only earth and sky,
the immensity of space, seemingly
limitless this openness, this emptiness
filled with life, and all are dwarfed by
faraway horizons that stretch beyond,
beckoning to follow, unbending roads
disappear in distance, haze the only
limit, colossal cumulonimbus clouds rise
twenty, thirty thousand feet into thinnest,
breathless air, and below grain silos
the highest human offering. Out there,
in endless expanse, there's healing there.

The Agendas of Sparrows

An early May morning,
and sparrows are busy
under eaves, flitting about,
twittering, at work with
agendas to feed and flourish,

air still cool and roads
yet empty, a sunny morning,
bright with color, the infinite
extent of blues and greens,
slight breezes brush tree tops.

In an hour, human sounds will
glaze the morning with disparate
agendas, getting and spending,
most assuming news inevitable,
forgetting the agendas of sparrows.

Climbing Trees

Trees were everywhere, across
the street a woods, mostly oak,
divided by an old rutted wagon
road, to the west a small apple
orchard, to the east a wooded
strip separating lots, in back
a small stand of pine, and the peach,
apricot, and cherry trees my parents
planted hopefully, and in front
the dogwood trees that blossomed,
a white silken canopy, every spring.
We climbed incessantly, heedless
insouciant boys, bark smudged,
sneakers straining footholds, small
hands grasping and grabbing, balancing
on thin branches, swinging, swaying,
daring, eyes squinting skyward, climbing
as high as we could go, never worrying
what held our weight, never imagining
that there was an end to higher,
that there was no higher to go,
or reckoning a risk of falling.

The Infinite Joy of Chasing Fireflies

A midsummer evening,
and in infinite twilight
children endlessly
chase fireflies, their
laughter lasting long
after nightfall, long
after the glimmer has
faded, even long after
lives have been lived.

Feathers and Wings

A feathery sky, distant clouds
mere wisps of wings high
in the empyrean blue, the bright
light of early spring, the earth
touched by green, a morning
poised on limitless promise.

Promising Forever But Not Another Day

We live acquainted with the knowing,
the dark approach, that dusk hovering
over the horizon, the ineluctable winter,
yet torn from time, never looking for that
never quite there. This late day, so sunlit
and cloudless, so serene, the bright blues
and greens of summer, though lost, still
linger, as shadows dance and laughter
echoes, this warmth entices and the breeze
beguiles, these late hours promise forever,
the always and evermore, but not another
day, these lovely days, so few, so stunning.

Even Darkness Spills Light

Winter's long and late to leave,
and an afternoon's walk is covered
in dusk and shadow, the sky's
sullen, choked with gray black clouds
that portend tomorrow's storm,
and a sharp wind stings, limiting
sight to ground, leash, and dog.

Yet walking requires glancing, three
buzzards rise, circling, then dart over
the creek bed, its steep bank eroded
by time, through the woods cantankerous
jays squawk, and in a thicket a squirrel
pokes and digs through dead leaves,
while a quick flash of cardinal startles.

When land is framed in darkness, winter
afternoons oppress, sealing despair as
shadows lengthen, yet ever there's
a certain slant of light that breaks
the cloud cover, revealing a glint of gold
in withered grass, a glimpse contracting
forever, and ever dog pulls leash
homeward. Even darkness spills light.